DIRECTOR'S CHOICE
**CATHEDRALS OF
THE CHURCH
OF ENGLAND**

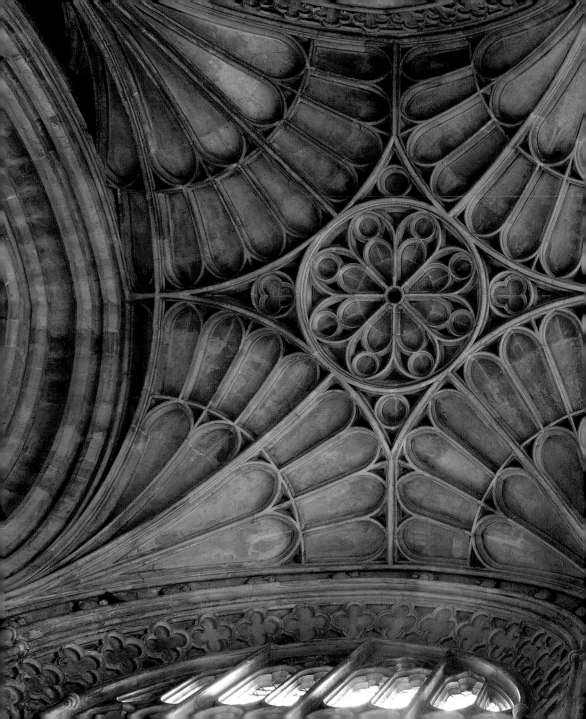

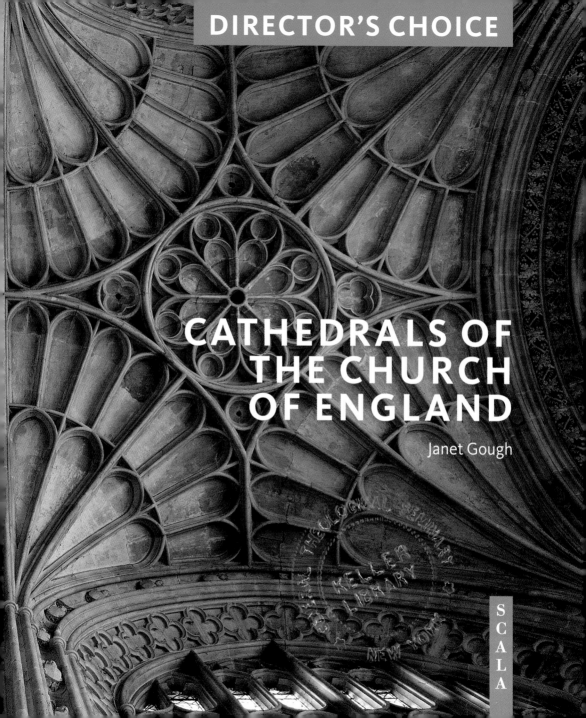

DIRECTOR'S CHOICE

CATHEDRALS OF
THE CHURCH
OF ENGLAND

Janet Gough

SCALA

INTRODUCTION

ENGLAND HAS NO FINER TREASURES than its cathedrals. They are awe-inspiring buildings whose magnificent architecture makes them great works of art in themselves. At the same time, our great cathedrals are unique repositories of our history. They are not just superb visual aids to understanding architectural history; so much of our social and communal as well as religious history is bound up with them. However, cathedrals are not art galleries or museums but living, breathing buildings which exist to serve God and the communities in which they stand. Many of them have been in continuous use for centuries and, in our own age, are more active than has even been the case in the past.

Standing at the heart of our cities, cathedrals are centres of prayer and culture in which glorious music to match their soaring architecture is offered at worship each day. They are open seven days a week for worship, mission, education and welcome to pilgrims and other visitors. In 2011 the Church of England's 42 cathedrals received over eleven million visitors – as many as English Heritage's 420 properties over the same period.

Jesus taught us to love God and neighbour so, alongside the worship and welcome they offer, cathedrals seek to reach out to people in their communities. They actively engage with the disenfranchised, the out-of-work, the elderly and the disabled, as can be seen, for example, at Portsmouth's Cathedral Innovation Centre. Several cathedrals are involved with inner city regeneration: for example, Blackburn's new

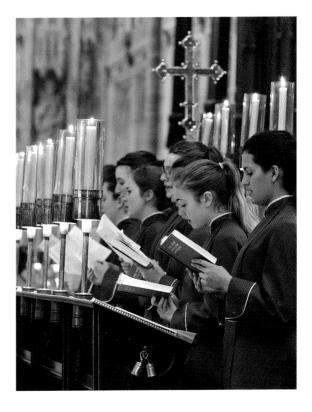

ABOVE: Girl choristers, Winchester Cathedral.

PREVIOUS PAGES: Fan vaulting in the Lady Chapel at Canterbury Cathedral.

multi-million pound Cathedral Quarter which is being created by the local council and businesses, with the cathedral at its centre.

The fact that cathedrals have stood four-square for lasting values at the heart of their cities for generations means that they are the natural focus for celebration and memorial in national life. This has been seen recently in the commemoration of the centenary of the outbreak of the First World War. Some cathedrals have a particular ministry in this area: Liverpool Cathedral, partly built during the First World War, has a purpose-built memorial chapel in which the then bishop's son, who was awarded two Victoria Crosses, is commemorated. Coventry Cathedral, its original medieval building destroyed during the Second World War, is dedicated to reconciliation.

BELOW: Scissor arches (1338–48) at Wells Cathedral.

Peter Ackroyd points out in his masterly account of the origins of the English imagination, *Albion*, that 'The notion of Englishness was a religious one from the moment Pope Gregory sent Augustine to England with the mission of establishing a Church of the English, in the light of his celebrated remark "non Angli sed angeli".' ('Not Angles but angels.') In cathedrals, faith and all that is best in English culture continue to meet. As the novelist Susan Hill asks: 'Where else in the heart of a city is such a place, where the sense of all past, all present, is distilled into the eternal moment "at the still point of the turning world"?'

Our cathedrals are a unique and very precious part of our heritage and ongoing national life which this book celebrates wonderfully. I hope you will enjoy it.

THE RT REVD DR JOHN INGE,
BISHOP OF WORCESTER
The Church of England's lead bishop for cathedrals and church buildings

CATHEDRALS OF THE CHURCH OF ENGLAND

A cathedral is the mother church of a diocese, the seat of a bishop. Together, the 42 English cathedrals of the Church of England constitute one of the world's great architectural achievements. They are an artistic embodiment of the spiritual sublime as well as a unique record of the history of the nation.

The management of the Church, divided into geographical dioceses each overseen by a bishop, was established along Roman lines following St Augustine of Canterbury's arrival on these shores in the late sixth century. Remarkably, it has persisted to the present day.

There are very few cathedral buildings surviving from the Dark Ages, St Wilfrid's Anglo-Saxon crypt at Ripon Cathedral being an exception. This is mostly a result of the huge cathedral rebuilding programme following the conquest of England in 1066 by William of Normandy. To make his mark, William the Conqueror had castles and quickly thereafter substantial cathedrals built in the strategic cities of England. This is why some dioceses were moved at this time, such as from Thetford to Norwich. It is incredible to think of the impact the great Norman cathedrals like Durham, with its high thick stone walls and massive cylindrical columns and round-topped arches, would have had on the local population.

By the mid-twelfth century, most of these great buildings were completed. About half the medieval cathedrals were monastic foundations, mostly of the great Benedictine order, ruled by an abbot bishop. By this time the Gothic style was emerging, strongly influenced from France. Its characteristics were pointed arches, even greater emphasis on soaring heights, thinner, pierced walls and light penetrating the building, often coloured through magnificent new stained-glass windows.

Salisbury Cathedral, built over 38 years from 1220, is the first complete cathedral in the new Early English Gothic style. Over time tracery in the windows and other decorative features became more complicated and curvilinear, evolving into what is called the Decorated style, a superb example of which is Exeter Cathedral.

This was followed by the Perpendicular style, a development

OPPOSITE: Lady Chapel at Liverpool Cathedral, by Sir Giles Gilbert Scott, consecrated in 1910.

unique to England, which involved decorative schemes based on grids of vertical and horizontal lines crossing surfaces and windows and creating a surface uniformity never seen before. We see its first stirrings in the presbytery of Gloucester Cathedral and its extraordinary crowning glory in the fan vaulting displayed in Gloucester's cloisters, the vault in Canterbury's Bell Harry Tower and the pendant-lierne vault in the choir of Christ Church, Oxford.

The huge shakeup of the Reformation in the early sixteenth century could have signalled an end to cathedrals. Instead King Henry VIII refounded the churches of some recently dissolved monasteries as new cathedrals, such as Peterborough and Gloucester.

Then followed the remarkable construction of St Paul's, England's first Protestant cathedral, ironically in the Baroque style. The Church of England has relatively few baroque churches, partly because the style had too strongly Catholic connotations. But Sir Christopher Wren was the supreme master who built to his own design in spite of the constraints put upon him.

Since then the Church has built or created new cathedrals in the idiom of the eighteenth century (Derby and Birmingham), the Victorian Gothic Revival (Truro) and three new cathedrals in the twentieth

LEFT: Henry VIII depicted in the Chichester Cathedral charter histories. Oil on panel by Lambert Barnard, 1533–37.

ABOVE: St Paul's
Cathedral, with
the City of London
skyscape beyond.

century: Liverpool and Guildford, both built in the Gothic tradition, and finally post-war Coventry Cathedral. From when they were first built, cathedral chapters have carried out major repairs and added fine new additions to their cathedrals, like Ely's Lady Chapel and the extraordinary Octagon of the mid-1300s.

Cathedrals house an unparalleled Christian material culture. In the medieval period most of them were highly painted and decorated. This decoration included marble, mosaics, wall paintings and encaustic tiles (extensive medieval tiling remains at the east end of Winchester) and, most visibly, stained glass, from the 1220 narrative windows at Canterbury to the gravity-defying Perpendicular east window of Gloucester. Figurative and decorative sculpture was highly significant, and in spite of the destruction wrought under Henry VIII, Edward VI and later Oliver Cromwell, magnificent examples survive. These are often located outside the church building, as in the chapter houses, the great boardrooms of the Middle Ages, such as the frieze at Salisbury with its Viking ship Noah's Ark and the extraordinarily naturalistic Leaves of Southwell.

Cathedrals were also great places of pilgrimage. St Thomas Becket's shrine at Canterbury was the most visited in north-western Europe, and it is interesting to see the revival of interest in shrines and reliquaries, evident in Hereford Cathedral. Cathedrals have been places of safe deposit and preserve six early versions of Magna Carta, two from 1215 (Lincoln and Salisbury). Music with attendant organs and bells plays a huge role, from the daily liturgical round to great works like Benjamin Britten's *War Requiem*, composed for Coventry Cathedral. And finally new art commissions are everywhere, from liturgical essentials such as William Pye's font at Salisbury (2008) to Bill Viola's powerful *Martyrs* video installation at St Paul's Cathedral (2014).

Mother church of Anglican Christianity worldwide

Canterbury Cathedral

England's first cathedral, founded by St Augustine in 597
www.canterbury-cathedral.org

SENT BY POPE GREGORY to convert pagan Saxon England to Christianity, St Augustine established a cathedral here under the protection of King Ethelbert. Following a fire in 1067, it was rebuilt by the first Norman archbishop, Lanfranc, using a similar design to St Etienne's Abbey in Caen, France, where he had previously been abbot, and importing stone from the same area that supplies the cathedral masons today.

The murder of Archbishop Thomas Becket in 1170, followed by a fire in 1174, led to the transformation of the cathedral. William of Sens designed a new choir and his successor William the Englishman created extensions eastwards to accommodate the tens of thousands of pilgrims flocking from across Europe.

The immense wealth of Becket's shrine was plundered under Henry VIII, but I was still struck by the sense of pilgrimage created by the stepped nature of the interior: progressing from the west door towards the high altar and choir, you have to climb steeply up, as if the building itself is urging you to your knees.

Up steps beyond the choir, St Augustine's Chair sits in solitary splendour. The only complete marble throne surviving from medieval England, this massive seat has been central to the installation ceremonies for Archbishops of Canterbury for 700 years.

A significant proportion of the cathedral's exquisite and very early twelfth- and thirteenth-century stained glass survived the iconoclasm of the Reformation and the Puritans; the largest collection is in the widest window of the cathedral, the great south window, where a £2.25 million programme of conservation is due to complete in 2015.

ABOVE: 'Adam Delving' (stained glass, 1176).

RIGHT: The high altar with St Augustine's Chair beyond.

St Augustine of Canterbury's second cathedral

Rochester Cathedral

Established by St Augustine in 604
www.rochestercathedral.org

ROCHESTER IS A RELATIVELY SMALL cathedral with a grand history. It was one of two dioceses established by St Augustine himself in AD 604, seven years after he arrived in Canterbury. Almost nothing survives of this original church, but the majority of the present Norman nave is that built by Bishop Gundulf in 1083, at the same time as the castle, which stands strikingly close to the cathedral today – a clear symbol of joint religious and civic power.

The twelfth-century west door to the cathedral (opposite) is decorated with high-relief carvings including the figures of Solomon, prefiguring Christ, and the Queen of Sheba. The choir and east end were built in the Early English Gothic style during the late twelfth and early thirteenth centuries. In the choir is a thirteenth-century wheel of fortune painting, of which half remains in an excellent state, depicting the rise of man from the depths to the height of success, while Fortune stands at the centre,

ABOVE: Church and State in the grip of William the Conqueror.

controlling the rotation. Another deeply and elaborately carved doorway, this time within a Decorated ogee arch of the 1340s, leads off the south-east transept to the library.

The Garth gardens to the south of the cathedral occupy the site of the old monastic cloister, and the remains of the twelfth-century chapter house, dormitory and refectory surround the rose garden. Rochester High Street runs almost immediately to the north of the cathedral, and to the north-east Chertsey's Gate remains as a reminder of the old monastic wall that divided the tranquil monastery property from the busy town.

Royal capital and resting place of Saxon monarchs

Winchester Cathedral

Established around 642, possibly as a royal chapel, and made a cathedral in the 660s
www.winchester-cathedral.org.uk

AS BEFITS THE CITY that was a seat of royal and ecclesiastical power in the Saxon period, the Middle Ages, and nearly under Charles II, Winchester Cathedral is imposing and well endowed. The present building is the longest medieval church surviving in Europe.

A plan of the Saxon minster, built near the site of the former Roman civic centre, is laid out in the grass north of the nave. From 1079 the minster was replaced by a much bigger Norman church, best appreciated today in the north transept and in the crypt, where a single figure sculpted by Antony Gormley stands, often knee-deep in water. Every later period added further architectural feats and delights, notably the ambitious remodelling of the Norman nave (opposite), partly achieved by recladding in the Perpendicular style. The six spectacular chantry chapels include one dedicated to the man behind these works, William of Wykeham, a fifteenth-century bishop of humble origins who founded both New College Oxford and Winchester College.

ABOVE: Historiated initial (a capital letter illustrating a Bible story) from the Winchester Bible, late twelfth century.

The cathedral's treasures and decoration enliven this magnificent space: from the twelfth century the black Tournai marble font carved with stories from the legend of St Nicholas, including the 'pickled boys' murdered by an innkeeper, and wall paintings of the deposition and entombment of Christ in the chapel of the Holy Sepulchre. New art is still being commissioned, most recently tapestry altar frontals for the high altar by Maggi Hambling.

The world-renowned Winchester Bible, created by one scribe and several peripatetic artists in the 1160s, is being re-displayed in a permanent exhibition, *Kings and Scribes: The Birth of a Nation*, alongside the results of an investigation into the cathedral's Renaissance mortuary chests containing the remains of late Anglo-Saxon kings.

Home to Elgar, the Three Choirs Festival and royal burials

Worcester Cathedral

Founded in 680

www.worcestercathedral.co.uk

WHEN I VISITED Worcester Cathedral the air was full of Sir Edward Elgar's *The Apostles* in rehearsal for the Three Choirs Festival. Held since 1715 in turn at Worcester, Hereford and Gloucester cathedrals, this is the oldest choral festival in the world.

Worcester has a spectacular setting, standing majestically above the River Severn. It was from the top of the tower that Charles II watched the battle of Worcester.

Recycled Saxon columns are set in the prior's parlour adjacent to the earliest circular chapter house which dates from 1100. These are two of the rare ensemble of monastic buildings which includes the Edgar tower, College hall and cloisters. The exquisite crypt of the Norman church, with its many aisles and rows of columns, is reminiscent of the cathedral-mosque of Cordoba. The cathedral itself enjoys a wonderful vista from east to west encompassing different architectural styles in one roof line.

King John's tomb stands directly in front of the high altar. Carved in Purbeck marble with two flanking saints, this is the earliest royal effigy in England. There's no effigy however for Prince Arthur, the elder brother of King Henry VIII, who died in nearby Ludlow shortly after marrying Katharine of Aragon and whose chantry chapel stands nearby.

Henry VIII's men did not get to plunder the monks' library during the Dissolution of the Monasteries. So Worcester Cathedral Library, high in the triforium, continues to house a glorious array of early manuscripts and books including King John's will, an early Caxton printed version of Chaucer's *The Reeve's Tale*, and music by Elgar.

ABOVE: The cathedral from across the River Severn.

OPPOSITE: The tomb of King John, who died in 1216.

World heritage site, the most impressive Norman church in England

Durham Cathedral

Established in 995 to shelter the remains of St Cuthbert; Norman cathedral built 1093–1133
www.durhamcathedral.co.uk

TOWERING ABOVE ITS CITY, the vastness of Durham Cathedral can be seen in the distance from the East Coast main railway line running north to Scotland. Close up, the awe-inspiring setting, high on a rocky outcrop encircled by the river and next to the castle, frames one of the finest Norman buildings in Europe.

The cathedral was established in Durham in 995 by monks carrying St Cuthbert's bones away from Lindisfarne in the wake of Norse invasion. The present Romanesque building, built by Benedictines, was begun in 1093 and replaced the earlier Saxon cathedral. It was finished in only 40 years and, internally at least, remains remarkably unaltered. It was originally built as a shrine, and many still make the journey of pilgrimage today, with daily prayers and services held over Cuthbert's grave.

The most striking features on entering Durham are the pillars, carved with deeply incised designs including chevrons and diamonds. In Durham we see the earliest pointed arch and ribbed vault in western Christian architecture, a hint of the full-blown Gothic style to come. The late twelfth-century Galilee Chapel at the west end, with its chevron arches and slender Purbeck piers, is the burial place for the Venerable Bede, the father of English history, and serves as the cathedral's Lady Chapel (more usually found at the east end). The mid-fourteenth-century stone reredos was donated by Lord Neville, carved in London and brought up by sea. Despite the removal of its statues at the Reformation, it remains imposing.

Durham's *Open Treasure* project will display the relics of St Cuthbert, alongside other treasures of the cathedral including the seventh-century Durham Gospels and three versions of Magna Carta, in the former monastery's Great Kitchen, a remarkable fourteenth-century octagonal space with a steeply vaulted ceiling.

ABOVE: March 1300 version of Magna Carta, Durham Cathedral.

OPPOSITE: Looking east up the nave, flanked by carved pillars and topped by its pioneering ribbed vault.

The ship of the fens, with extraordinary Decorated inventiveness

Ely Cathedral

Founded as a monastery by St Ethelreda and made a cathedral in 1083
www.elycathedral.org

BEDE TELLS US that St Ethelreda, princess and abbess, established and presided over a monastery for men and women in Ely in 673. This was eventually superseded by a great Benedictine monastery, to which her shrine was transferred. The Norman abbey is still visible in the vast nave built from the 1080s onwards, together with the heavily arcaded south arm of the west front and the intricate Romanesque carving over the Prior's and monks' doors.

Ely Cathedral is visible across the flat fens from miles around. The octagon and lantern rising out of the crossing are spectacular and unique. Built between 1322 and 1340 following the collapse of the crossing tower, the octagonal tower, with its painted wooden vaulting and soaring upright lantern, is a triumph of medieval engineering and aesthetics. Sir Christopher Wren's uncle was Bishop of Ely in the mid-seventeenth century and Wren must have taken inspiration for the dome of St Paul's Cathedral from Ely's octagon.

The superlative Lady Chapel was also built in the fourteenth century. It is a stunning example of the most advanced Decorated Gothic style of architecture. Look beyond the systematic ravages of the Reformation iconoclasts and enjoy the nodding ogee forms of the hooded chapter seats, the swaying figure forms and minutely decorated surfaces.

For many years the Lady Chapel was a separate parish church. Recently it was re-linked with the cathedral via an understated building, following the old processional way. It was designed by Jane Kennedy, who has also installed a new floor and introduced a contemporary reredos and altar in the Lady Chapel. St Ethelreda might be pleased to know the church built on her foundation flourishes under the watchful eye of a female architect and a female clerk of works.

ABOVE: The Norman west end was complete by 1189, with the central tower between western transepts. The north-west transept collapsed in the fifteenth century. The Galilee porch of *c.*1200 and the top stage of the tower, 1500s, were added later.

OPPOSITE: The great octagon and lantern from below.

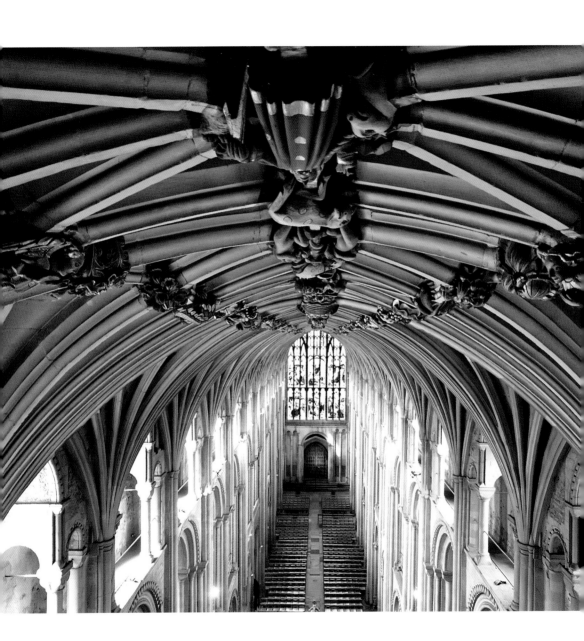

Norman building with late Gothic vaulting, spire and bosses

Norwich Cathedral

Founded by the Normans in 1096
www.cathedral.org.uk

THE NORMANS MOVED the diocese in East Anglia to Norwich and characteristically built a fort and then a cathedral. The Romanesque cathedral, with its original apsidal or semi-circular east end, still stands at the centre of this market town. In later centuries the cloister was rebuilt (1297–1430) and the monks entered the cathedral via the lavishly carved Prior's Door. The whole cathedral was vaulted in stone and a late Gothic spire was built.

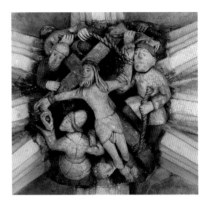

ABOVE: A ceiling boss depicting the Crucifixion.

The lierne rib vaulting sits surprisingly harmoniously on the earlier round-arched walls and is decorated by a remarkably preserved collection of over 400 coloured ceiling bosses (opposite). These circular carved and painted bosses tell the story of the Creation at the east end, the Last Judgement at the west, and the Apocalypse in the fine two-storey cloisters.

An ambulatory circles the presbytery at the east end and slopes gently down to evoke a circular crypt, at the easternmost point on which is a large niche, designed to hold saints' relics. This has a flue connecting it to the ancient bishop's throne above, presumably to ensure the holy fumes were appropriately directed. Off the ambulatory Bishop Dispenser's five-panelled altarpiece of 1380 is painted and gilded in the gorgeous international Gothic style and is one of the cathedral's great treasures.

More recently the monks' Benedictine hospitality has been revived through the building of first the refectory and then the hostry in the ruins of the equivalent buildings in the medieval monastery. These buildings, designed by Michael Hopkins, are a noble twenty-first-century addition to one of our most exquisite cathedral buildings.

Cathedral showing its scars and delighting in its riches

Carlisle Cathedral

Part-destroyed Norman cathedral from 1133, with Victorian and later additions
www.carlislecathedral.org.uk

FOUNDED AS AN AUGUSTINIAN PRIORY by Henry I in 1122, Carlisle's modest footprint is mainly because all but two bays of its original seven-bay Norman nave were destroyed during the English Civil War, demolished by the Scottish Presbyterian Army in order to use the stone to reinforce Carlisle Castle. This great architectural tragedy doesn't detract from what remains: heroic Norman transepts and a Decorated choir and presbytery.

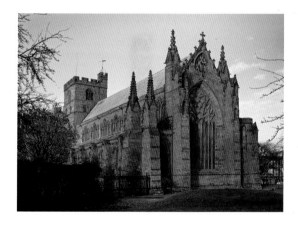

The mid-fourteenth-century east window, with its flowing tracery and medieval glass in the top lights, and the painted ceiling (a Victorian reconstruction, shown opposite) create a magnificent chancel space. Around the chancel, fourteenth-century capitals depict the Labours of the Month, illuminating the annual cycle of the medieval farmer.

Between 1853 and 1870 Carlisle Cathedral was restored by Ewan Christian. It was at this time that the new principal entrance was created in the south transept façade. Following this programme of restoration other notable architects also turned their hand to Carlisle, including G. E. Street, Stephen Dykes Bower and Sir Charles Nicholson.

OPPOSITE: The painted chancel ceiling.

The cathedral precinct, an important green space and thoroughfare used by locals, encloses the medieval Fratry with its vaulted undercroft and the fifteenth-century Prior's Tower which boasts a solar or dayroom with a brightly coloured, panelled and painted ceiling.

One of the largest medieval Gothic buildings,
with extensive medieval glass

York Minster

Present cathedral built from 1080
www.yorkminster.org

BUILT OVER A ROMAN FORTRESS and Anglo-Saxon cemetery, the imposing minster represents all periods of Gothic architecture with its Early English transepts, Decorated chapter house and nave, and Perpendicular east end. It also retains remains of the original Romanesque building.

The minster boasts more medieval glass than any other church in England; it was saved from destruction in the English Civil War by parliamentary general Lord Fairfax. The Five Sisters window, dating from the 1230s, has tall lancet windows characteristic of Early English architecture, which are filled with an abstract pattern of grisaille glass of a greenish-grey hue, and dominates the north transept. Most remarkable is the great east window of 1405–08, the largest expanse of medieval glass in the world. Created by John Thornton, the foremost glazier of his day, it comprises 117 panels in rows of nine crowned by flowing tracery. God as Alpha and Omega sits on the top, above scenes from Genesis, the beginning, and Revelation, the end. The window has been the focus of a major conservation and interpretation programme which also produced an excellent interpretative museum in the undercroft and new gargoyles from the stonemasons' yard high up on the east end (inside back cover).

In the thirteenth century, the Chapter built the largest octagonal chapter house in England to rival those of Westminster Abbey and Salisbury. Unusually, it has no central pier, as its vaulted roof is of wood rather than stone. The chapter house was a kind of medieval boardroom: a speaker standing in front of his or her seat can still be heard perfectly without amplification. Here Edward I and II held parliaments during their Scottish campaigns. York Minster remains the seat of the Archbishop of York, the second highest office-holder in the Church of England.

ABOVE: God as Alpha and Omega, *c.*1400, atop the great east window.

OPPOSITE: The distinctive curvilinear tracery of the great west window, 1330s, dominates the west front.

The tallest building in the medieval world

Lincoln Cathedral

One of our finest Gothic buildings, with a great Norman west front; consecrated 1092
www.lincolncathedral.com

COMMISSIONED BY WILLIAM THE CONQUEROR shortly after his post-conquest military promenade of England, Lincoln Cathedral is visible for miles around with its three tall towers facing the castle. The Norman west front remains, but after an earthquake in 1185 Bishop Hugh of Avalon rebuilt the cathedral on an even grander scale, in the new Gothic style.

Lincoln's masons produced extraordinarily high vaults, including the staggered or 'crazy' vaults in the choir which appear to be deliberately asymmetric. Later the crossing tower was built to a height of 270 feet and topped with a thin spire said to have been as long as the completed church and higher than the Great Pyramid of Giza in Egypt, making it the tallest building in the world between 1311 and 1548, when it collapsed, and demonstrating to medieval onlookers that Christ's Church was superior to anything the ancients could achieve.

The wide west screen of Lincoln, inspired by Constantine's Arch in Rome, and built between 1075 and 1092, is impressive from afar and close up, with its three deep recesses, long horizontal lined arcading and carved friezes, secured at each end by polygonal turrets with spires. Inside, huge round traceried windows in the principal transepts and the carved angels of the Angel Choir (1256–80) also delight. The cloisters lead to Lincoln's chapter house and to the library over the north walk which was rebuilt by Sir Christopher Wren.

ABOVE: The centrally planned, thirteenth-century decagonal chapter house; its pyramid-shaped roof is visible to the left of the cathedral in the photograph opposite.

Those of us who as teenagers adored Anya Seton's book *Katherine* will be interested that from 1381 Katherine Swynford, sister-in-law of Geoffrey Chaucer, rented the Chancery, now the Deanery, and that with her daughter she is buried in the cathedral. She was the mistress of the powerful John of Gaunt, whom she eventually married, producing a family whose descendants became our Tudor kings.

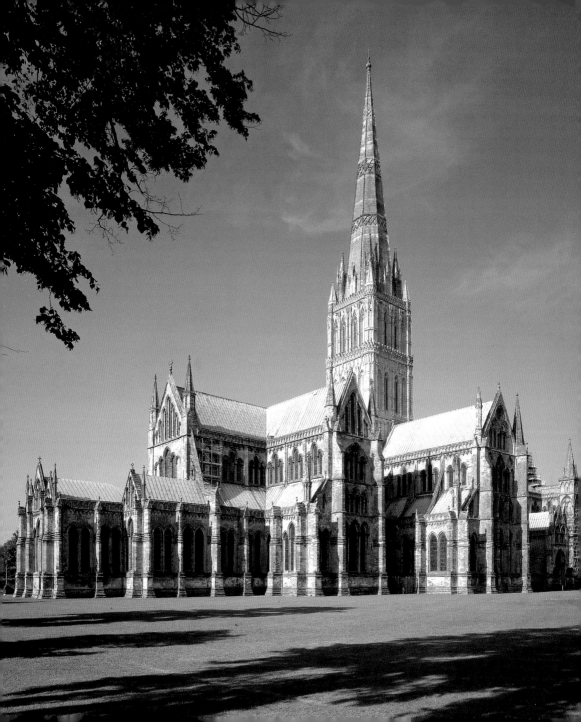

Early English Gothic cathedral with England's tallest spire, painted by Constable

Salisbury Cathedral

Constructed 1220–1258 in the Early English Gothic style
www.salisburycathedral.org.uk

In 1220 A BRAND-NEW CATHEDRAL was commissioned when the bishop moved his community from the hill of Old Sarum to a meadow beside the river Avon. Salisbury Cathedral is unusual in England for being built over 38 years in one style, Early English Gothic. Clusters of two, three and even seven lancet windows cover the exterior of the cathedral. Inside, the long clear view from west to east of continuous arcading is picked out by Purbeck marble piers.

At the same time a wide cloister and octagonal chapter house were constructed. The chapter house is decorated with a lively carved frieze depicting stories from Genesis and Exodus in fascinating thirteenth-century idiom, including a Viking-shaped boat as Noah's ark.

A century later the crossing tower was crowned with the tallest tower and spire in England. Medieval and later engineering continues to support the spire, which has been painted by John Constable and many others and remains emblematic of the cathedral.

ABOVE: William Pye's font, with the nave beyond.

With one of the four surviving 1215 copies of Magna Carta permanently on display (Lincoln Cathedral owns another), the cathedral continues to emphasise its role in supporting social and political justice, witnessed in the deep-blue Prisoner of Conscience Window at the far east end Trinity Chapel, the Amnesty International candle and the Sudan Chapel.

William Pye's 2008 font, with its smooth infinity-pool-style water surface, offers a liturgical welcome as you enter the cathedral, and is a powerful message that the cathedral is a living place of new beginnings.

Ancient cathedral exhibiting the full glories of the Decorated style

Exeter Cathedral

A cathedral since 1050 (the Norman towers remain); mostly built 1275–1375.
www.exeter-cathedral.org.uk

ALMOST COMPLETELY REPLACING an earlier Norman cathedral, a new cathedral in the sprightly Decorated Gothic style was built between 1275 and 1375. The resulting nave is a delightfully unified space where the pillars contrive to be both massive and delicately fluted, and the stone ribs of the roof, like branches of an avenue of tall trees, form the longest uninterrupted medieval vaulted ceiling in the world.

OPPOSITE: Looking east past the bishop's throne (shown at right).

BELOW: Tomb of Walter Bronescombe, Bishop of Exeter 1258–80. Black basalt effigy with later canopy and base.

The nave is separated from the choir by a low stone pulpitum with cusped and crocketed ogee arches. Above this sits the 1665 organ which was re-installed following a £1 million restoration in 2014. The choir has a very early collection of misericord carvings, including one of an elephant, apparently kept by King Henry III in the Tower of London. Miraculously saved from war damage, the magnificent 60-foot early fourteenth-century cathedra or bishop's throne (see opposite) is a virtuoso study in Decorated Gothic with nodding ogees, gables and a pierced spire. Carved in Devon oak it demonstrates the skills of the wood sculptor.

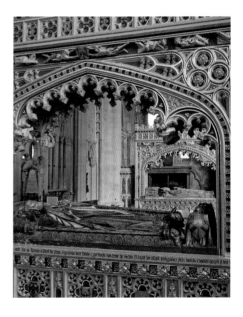

Outside, an image screen with rows of statues, originally brightly coloured, was installed across almost the full width of the west front between *c.* 1340 and 1470. At the apex of the gable stands Simon Verity's 1985 sculpture depicting St Peter as a young fisherman, stripped and ready for action.

Adjacent to significant Roman remains and owning both the Anglo-Saxon Exeter Book, which is arguably the oldest book of English literature, and William the Conqueror's Exon Domesday survey for the Exeter area, the cathedral engages with nearly 2000 years of history.

'The most typical English cathedral' – Sir Nikolaus Pevsner

Chichester Cathedral

Founded as one of William the Conqueror's stone cathedrals in 1076
www.chichestercathedral.org.uk

CHICHESTER CATHEDRAL reveals a long period of almost continuous development; with evidence of work of every century since its Norman foundation. It is a good place to follow stylistic development, such as the transition from use of the round to the pointed arch, which is clearly visible in the retrochoir.

Relations with the monarchy, good and not so good, are well demonstrated at Chichester. King John is reputed to have donated the Purbeck marble piers in the nave. In the transepts the newly conserved painted panels of the 1530s by Lambert Barnard depict kings of England and historic events on a large scale: one shows Bishop Sherburne pleading with Henry VIII, who probably wasn't actually there, to respect the cathedral as the king embarked on his Reformation of the Church (illustrated on page 8). In the north transept, a century later, a monument was created to John Cawley and his son: the father signed Charles I's death warrant and his son took on his father's status as 'unexempted' from the crime of regicide, becoming a wanted man under the restored Charles II.

More recently the cathedral has become known as a place of reconciliation, particularly so under courageous Bishop Bell who, while not a pacifist, encouraged international understanding and provided refuge for political dissidents from Germany in the 1930s. Under Bishop Bell, Walter Hussey was appointed as Dean. Dean Hussey was responsible for a remarkable series of mid-twentieth-century furnishings and fine art commissions. These include John Piper's bold, colourful tapestry hanging behind the high altar and Marc Chagall's striking stained-glass window celebrating the joys of life from the words of Psalm 150.

Unusually for English cathedrals, Chichester also has a stand-alone sixteenth-century bell tower.

ABOVE: Stained-glass window by Marc Chagall, unveiled by the Duchess of Kent in 1978.

The Ladies of the Vale – and a local saint

Lichfield Cathedral

Ancient shrine of St Chad; a cathedral since 1048
www.lichfield-cathedral.org

KNOWN LOCALLY as 'the Ladies of the Vale', the three elegant spires of Lichfield Cathedral are an iconic sight. This is the only cathedral in England still with three spires. Built of red sandstone, it suffered during the Civil War but retains a grandeur in its beautiful close, which was originally moated. Lichfield is dedicated to St Chad, a seventh-century missionary to Mercia who became bishop here from 669 until his death in 672. Although it was known that there were Saxon and Norman churches on the site, no trace had been found of them until works were done to install a new altar platform in 2003. While digging down, a remarkable carved limestone panel depicting an angel was uncovered. It was later decided that this was the lid of a shrine chest, possibly even that of St Chad, and dated to around 800.

The cathedral we see today is mainly thirteenth-century and represents, in the nave at least, some of the earliest of the Decorated style of architecture. The polygonal chapter house (1249) displays the Angel and the eighth-century St Chad's Gospels alongside Saxon treasures from the Staffordshire Hoard.

The Civil War was a testing time for Lichfield: the Dean and Chapter of the cathedral declared themselves firmly royalist whilst the town was parliamentarian. Despite fortifying the close, the cathedral fell to the town and was badly damaged in the ensuing rampage. Restoration was assured by King Charles II and Bishop Hacket. Today the sixteenth-century Herkenrode glass, installed in 1805 and newly revealed in 2015, sparkles through Sir George Gilbert Scott's lacy screen at the end of the long stone choir.

ABOVE: The Lichfield Angel, *c.*800.

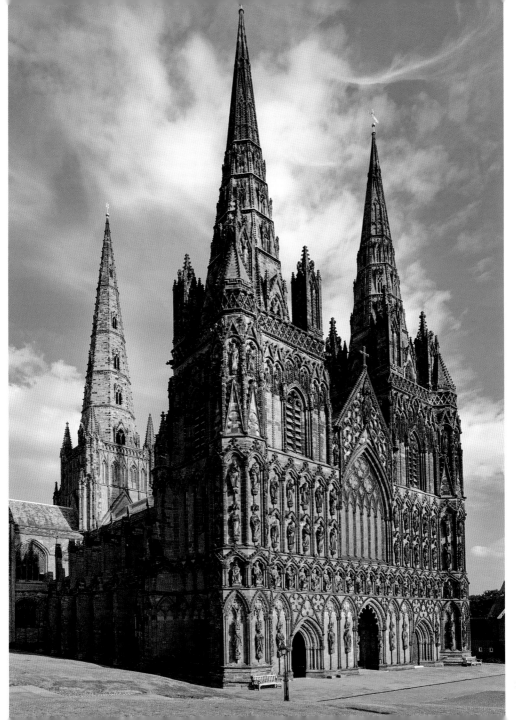

New cathedral, replacing Bath,
with much inventive Gothic design and detailing

Wells Cathedral

Gothic cathedral constructed over 250 years from 1175
www.wellscathedral.org.uk

A CHURCH HAS EXISTED beside the natural spring, 'Wells', since the early eighth century. The Normans sited the diocese in Bath, but it was moved to Wells in 1219 and work on a new cathedral began: first the west front with its extraordinary array of nearly 300 medieval sculptures in little aedicules (small buildings), the north porch with its pointed-arch doorway and the nave with an arcade of lancets piercing the triforium. In the late 1200s a cloister and a chapter house were added. Unusually the chapter house was built over a ground-level crypt which housed a treasury and now tells the story of the cathedral. Wide and well worn golden stone steps gently curl up to the chapter house, the vicar's hall and chain bridge beyond. This leads to the Vicar's Close, the oldest continually inhabited street in Europe, built for the canons who serve Wells Cathedral.

Building works progressed into the east end, culminating in the great east window, a Jesse window which tells the story of Christ's birth and resurrection linked by curling tendrils to his ancestors, including Jesse, the father of David. The golds, greens, reds and blues of this newly conserved window glitter like precious gemstones. Beyond is the Lady Chapel in the rare form of a compressed octagon with an exquisite painted star vault of *c.*1320. In 1338, after alarming cracks began to appear around the tower, huge scissor arches (see page 5) were installed in the crossing to take the weight of the tower and former timber and lead spire.

In the fourteenth century a clock was installed in the north transept with a 24-hour painted clock face and a large oak figure who strikes his bell every quarter while jousting knights revolve. A century later a further clock face and striking figure in knight's armour were added to the external transept wall. Six hundred years on, the clock remains in excellent working order.

ABOVE: Well worn steps leading up to the chapter house, vicar's hall and chain bridge. This view was described by Sir Simon Jenkins as 'the loveliest sight in England'.

A place of pilgrimage and treasures

Hereford Cathedral

Ancient Norman cathedral begun in the first half of the twelfth century
www.herefordcathedral.org

HEREFORD HAS BEEN the centre of a diocese since 676. Its largely Norman fabric was tragically neglected during the eighteenth century and on Easter Monday 1786 the west tower collapsed, bringing down much of the west end. The nave was rebuilt, though two bays shorter, and the cathedral was made sound by later Victorians. It is a salutary lesson on the need for ongoing fabric maintenance.

There is much left of the Romanesque building with its fine carving. Most distinctive is Hereford's elegant central tower of *c*.1325, covered with ball flowers, a popular local architectural feature.

The central tower was funded through offerings from pilgrims visiting the shrine of St Thomas Cantilupe. Thomas, Bishop of Hereford 1275–82, was the last English saint to be canonised before the Reformation. His shrine of around 1287 has recently been restored and a brightly painted canopy added. When medieval pilgrims visited the shrine they also saw the Mappa Mundi, a map of the known world on vellum. It is the largest known map to have survived from the Middle

ABOVE: Mappa Mundi (1290–1300).

OPPOSITE: Shrine of St Thomas Cantilupe.

Ages. During a major financial crisis in the 1980s the Mappa Mundi was nearly sold, but is now on permanent display along with the cathedral's library of chained books, which include a 1217 Magna Carta and a 1215 King John's Writ (not always on display), in a purpose-built 1990s building adjoining the cloisters.

The magnificent Booth Porch, built in the early 1500s to receive pilgrims, remains the main entrance to the cathedral.

Resting place of two queens

Peterborough Cathedral

Twelfth-century Norman abbey; became a cathedral under Henry VIII
www.peterborough-cathedral.org.uk

PETERBOROUGH IS PERHAPS among the least visited of England's great medieval cathedrals, but its architectural glories include the three vast portico arches of the startling west front, and a coolly spacious Norman nave with a painted wooden ceiling, dating from 1230–50, a unique survival in Britain. It is hard to credit that its fantastic images framed by jazzy-looking decorated lozenges date from the early thirteenth century.

The remarkable Hedda Stone (*c.*800), an Anglo-Saxon carving depicting twelve figures, may have come from the first monastery on the site, sacked by the Danes in 870.

At the east end the New Building is a late fifteenth-century extension, probably built by the architect of King's College Chapel, Cambridge, and featuring the same intricate fan vaulting. The unusual watchtower of St Oswald's Chapel guarded a shrine housing the saint's arm; the relic was destroyed at the Reformation. The church itself survived to become one of the new cathedrals created by Henry VIII to improve the balance between population and diocese size, with the abbot becoming the first Bishop of Peterborough.

Henry VIII's uneasy conscience may have been another reason that ensured Peterborough's relative good fortune: his discarded wife Katharine of Aragon had recently been buried with great ceremony at the abbey, in 1536. Her tomb was destroyed in the Civil War but a new memorial was installed in the late nineteenth century following a public appeal by a wife of one of the cathedral canons, herself a Katharine. Peterborough Cathedral was also the burial place for Mary, Queen of Scots after her execution in 1587, until her son James I had her body re-interred in Westminster Abbey. A portrait of 'Old Scarlett', the long-lived gravedigger who buried both queens, is at the west end.

OPPOSITE: Fan vaulting, *c.*1496–1508, probably designed by John Wastell who went on to work on King's College Chapel in Cambridge.

Wolsey's college chapel and the city's cathedral

Christ Church Cathedral, Oxford

Norman convent and church; raised to cathedral status in 1546
www.chch.ox.ac.uk/cathedral

FOUNDED AS A CONVENT by local saint St Frideswide some 1300 years ago, today's church was built in the twelfth century and later became an Augustinian priory and place of pilgrimage. In 1525, Henry VIII's right-hand man Cardinal Wolsey suppressed the priory of Frideswide and began work on creating a college on the site, to be named Cardinal's College in his honour. With great speed he commissioned a huge classical quadrangle, which necessitated knocking down the three western bays of the church. The plan was to construct a vast chapel – as at King's College, Cambridge – on one side of the quad.

ABOVE: Lierne vaulting with stone pendants (mid-fifteenth century).

However, after Wolsey's fall from power the remaining church was preserved by Henry VIII and the college re-founded as Christ Church. We can still enjoy the core Norman building with its impressive double arches and the spectacular Perpendicular Gothic vaulted ceiling over the choir. The lierne ribs create star patterns across the vault and are finished off with gravity-defying stone pendants. This late Gothic *tour de force* is one of the great achievements of the Perpendicular style, only to be found in England.

Among the remarkable stained glass is the Becket Window in St Lucy's Chapel, which dates from the mid-fourteenth century. It owes its survival to quick thinking that had the section depicting Thomas Becket's face replaced with plain glass when Henry VIII ordered the destruction of all representations of the 'turbulent priest'.

Established as both a cathedral and a college chapel, Christ Church uniquely retains that dual status.

A textbook in medieval architecture,
with the earliest stirrings of the Perpendicular style

Gloucester Cathedral

Great Norman abbey church; made a cathedral in 1541
www.gloucestercathedral.org.uk

GLOUCESTER'S ELEVATION to cathedral status was thanks in part to its royal connections, being the burial place both of William the Conqueror's eldest son Robert Curthose and of the murdered Edward II, whose shrine became a popular pilgrim destination.

The nave of Gloucester Cathedral is an architectural textbook with its solid Norman pillars, Early English vault, Decorated south aisle (with attractive ball-flower surface decoration) and the two west end bays in the Perpendicular style.

Edward III was determined his father should have a proper resting place, resulting in the remodelling of the south transept and presbytery from the 1330s in the extraordinary and brand new Perpendicular style. The angel vault crowning the presbytery is filled with carved figures proclaiming Christ in Majesty surrounded by angels. Equally spectacular is the immense east window. This wall of medieval glass is as large as a tennis court. Beyond that, the Lady Chapel is another handsome example of the Perpendicular style.

Today the muted colours of Tom Denny's stained-glass windows commemorating the life of local First World War poet and composer, Ivor Gurney, permeate through the screen of a chantry chapel into the Lady Chapel, reinforcing a spirit of contemplation.

OPPOSITE:
The Perpendicular great east window, *c.*1550, commemorates the English victory at Crécy in 1346.

Perhaps the most recognisable part of Gloucester, at least to younger visitors, is the early fan-vaulted cloisters (illustrated on the back cover), today famous as the corridors of Hogwarts in the *Harry Potter* films. Groups of schoolchildren can be seen darting around, creating their own stories in this cathedral steeped in history and inspirational art and architecture.

Architecturally arresting church becomes cathedral
for England's gateway to the New World

Bristol Cathedral

Twelfth-century Augustinian church; became one of Henry VIII's new cathedrals
www.bristol-cathedral.co.uk

THE SITE OF THE AUGUSTINIAN CHURCH founded by the first Lord
Berkeley in around 1140 became in time the civic heart of the city of
Bristol. Its Romanesque architecture, which can still be seen in the
richly decorated chapter house and abbey gatehouse, is among the
most lavishly inventive of the era, while the 'Harrowing of Hell', an
Anglo-Saxon carving discovered accidentally under the chapter house
floor, testifies to a well-established earlier Christian community. The
Elder Lady Chapel is a textbook work of Early English Gothic, full of
entertaining details, and possibly by the designer of
the west front of Wells Cathedral.

In the early fourteenth century the east end
of the church was rebuilt, paid for by the Berkeley
family, whose exuberant-looking starburst tombs line
the walls.

The nave and aisles are of the same
height, creating an unusual sense of
light and space. This design came to be
known as a hall church and was taken up in
continental Europe. Equally noteworthy is the east-
end decoration. In the Decorated Gothic style, it is full
of highly original elements including no capitals on the
arcade arches, inventive vaults springing from little bridges across
each aisle bay and of course the starburst tombs.

ABOVE: Starburst
ornamentation of
the Berkeley tombs
(fourteenth century) as
featured in the BBC's
Wolf Hall.

The church formally became a cathedral in 1542 after the abbey
was surrendered to Henry VIII's commissioners in 1539. Sadly the
medieval nave did not survive, and only in the late nineteenth century
was one finally provided, by Gothic Revival architect G. E. Street.
The architect of Truro Cathedral, John Loughborough Pearson,
completed the project.

The best-preserved group of monastic buildings in England

Chester Cathedral

Norman abbey church; created a cathedral by Henry VIII in 1541
www.chestercathedral.com

A CHURCH HAS EXISTED among the fortifications of Chester since 660. It is reputed to stand on a Roman temple site. In 1092 the church became the site of a great Romanesque Benedictine abbey, under the personal direction of St Anselm. Permanently created a cathedral in 1541, Chester retains an extensive and intact set of monastic buildings including the cloister, refectory and rectangular Early English chapter house. Work continued on the future cathedral during the medieval period, with a 130-year break between 1360 and 1490 because of the difficulties in recruiting workers after the Black Death.

The cathedral precinct still occupies around a quarter of the space within Chester's medieval city walls. Its pink sandstone glitters in the sunshine.

Today you can admire the building by taking a 'Cathedral at Heights' tour, giving the visitor the opportunity to look down the full length of the choir and nave from the clerestory passage above the altar, see up close George Pace's 1960s painted tower vault, walk over a stone vault, and look across the surrounding countryside from the crossing tower, as Charles I did when he watched his troops being defeated at the battle of Rowton Moor.

OPPOSITE: Nave view from the 'Cathedral at Heights' tour.

The remarkably conserved choir stalls and misericords from the late fourteenth century are a highlight. Exquisitely carved and still fresh, they provide vignettes into the daily life, real and imaginary, of the 1380s.

A baroque masterpiece

St Paul's Cathedral, London

The first Protestant cathedral in England, built in 1675–1710 following the Great Fire
www.stpauls.co.uk

'IF YOU REQUIRE A MONUMENT, look around you' reads the epitaph on the tomb of Sir Christopher Wren in the crypt of the cathedral he constructed. Wren's building replaced a significant medieval cathedral with increasing structural problems, finally destroyed by the Great Fire of London in 1666.

Up in the triforium is Wren's Great Model of 1674, planned to embody the Renaissance ideal of beauty as well as the perfection of God. But this design was rejected by clergy as untraditional and too Roman Catholic. Eventually a redesign was approved with the get-out clause 'to make some variations, rather ornamental than essential as from time to time he should see proper'. So over the next 35 years, paid for by the Coal Tax, Londoners acquired a cathedral in Gothic Latin cross plan with a restrained baroque cladding, crowned by a classical dome.

ABOVE: Wren's Great Model, his original design for the cathedral.

OPPOSITE: The geometric staircase.

Of course it is much more than that. Wren, one-time Professor of Astronomy at Oxford, produced the breathtaking cantilevered geometric staircase within the south-west tower, apparently designed to accommodate a vast telescope. Thanks to his royal connections, Wren employed a stellar group of artists and craftsmen to complete his church: Jean Tijou created the exquisite wrought iron grills, Grinling Gibbons the limewood carvings in the choir stalls, and Sir James Thornhill the grisaille *Life of St Paul* under a *trompe-l'oeil* colonnade in the dome (illustrated on the front cover flap). The Victorians considered Wren's cathedral to lack colour, and installed the colourful mosaics around the dome and east end.

The overall effect is dramatic, with light streaming down from heaven expressing the majesty of Almighty God. The inscription 'Resurgam' on the south transept façade expresses the 'rising again' of London, the Stuart monarchy and the cathedral itself, echoing down the ages the Christian resurrection faith in Jesus Christ.

Cradle of Christianity in northern England

Ripon Cathedral

Anglo-Saxon church; made a cathedral in 1836
www.riponcathedral.info

THIS COMPACT CATHEDRAL built in a grand style is also one of our oldest foundations. A stone church has existed in continuous use for nearly 1350 years since St Wilfrid founded an abbey here in 672. Visitors can still see the remarkably intact seventh-century crypt of his Anglo-Saxon church beneath the nave.

The striking west front, a fine example of Early English Gothic architecture from the 1220s, provides the iconic view of the cathedral from the grounds of the nearby Fountains Abbey, itself founded in the twelfth century by Ripon monks and now a world heritage site.

Having been an important minster church used by the archbishops of York, who resided in the adjacent manor, in 1836 Ripon became the first newly created cathedral church after the Reformation. In the intervening years the well-connected church benefitted from several ambitious rebuilds as well as occasional setbacks, so that changes in architectural style can be clearly observed. The nave was rebuilt in 1502 and the tall, uninterrupted cluster of piers that stop abruptly where the nave abuts the Norman crossing indicate how a grand Perpendicular church might have been continued.

ABOVE: Misericord of a man carrying timber, *c.*1490.

Beyond the carved pulpitum (whose figures, now replaced, were torn down by soldiers in the Civil War) with its magnificent organ above, the choir stalls of around 1490 are particularly fine, with 34 exquisite and amusing misericord carvings. Made by Ripon woodcarvers, they depict stories from the Bible or popular folklore and include a mermaid, a man carrying a heavy bundle of timber, and a rabbit disappearing down a hole. Lewis Carroll's father was a canon at Ripon Cathedral and the latter carving is thought to have inspired Carroll's *Alice in Wonderland*.

City-centre cathedral with a mission of hope

Manchester Cathedral

Fifteenth-century parish church; made a cathedral in 1847
www.manchestercathedral.org

MANCHESTER IS ONE OF the oldest of the new cathedrals, having been elevated from a collegiate church in 1847. The building itself is mainly fifteenth-century, and both the west end and the impressive choir screen remain from this period. It was considerably altered in the nineteenth century, including the addition of the western porch which, unusually, has steep steps leading up into the nave, giving visitors entering this way an arresting first impression.

All the Victorian stained glass was lost in a Second World War air raid in 1940, but has been replaced at both ends. In the west end a complete run of windows by Anthony Holloway dominates, and in the east end are a series of individual windows including the Fire Window by Margaret Traherne, remembering the 1940s Blitz, and the 2004 Healing Window commemorating the IRA bombing in central Manchester. These windows in some ways show the cathedral at its best – responding to tragedy with beauty and art.

The cathedral is very much a living, changing building, with one of the latest additions being the 2014 installation of a new underfloor heating system powered by eco-friendly ground source pumps. A major re-ordering of the nave and choir aisles was completed at the same time and now features a restored baptistery near the south porch. Right next door to the central shopping area, the cathedral is part of the regeneration of one of England's most vibrant cities.

OPPOSITE: Margaret Traherne's Fire Window, commemorating the Blitz, in the chapel of the Duke of Lancashire's Regiment.

Majestic Gothic Revival building with four spires, scaled to fit its site

Truro Cathedral

The first purpose-built cathedral church in a new diocese since the Middle Ages
www.trurocathedral.org.uk

THE CATHEDRAL CHURCH of St Mary, Truro is a Victorian Gothic church, built after the establishment of the diocese of Truro in 1876. It took seven years to build the first stage of the cathedral (the sanctuary and choir). The architect was John Loughborough Pearson, one of the finest ecclesiastical architects of the time. The cathedral became a family project, with the nave and the spires on the north-west tower being erected by Pearson's son in 1910. The First World War prevented the adding of cloisters, but the chapter house (now the cathedral restaurant) was added in 1967.

The cathedral was sited adjacent to an older church, part of which survives as the south side chapel. Internally there is an elaborate reredos, designed by the architect, and the world's largest stained-glass project on the history of the Church, by Clayton and Bell. It is an outstanding example of the Gothic Revival. Perhaps Pearson was conscious of the extreme youth of the diocese, contrasting it with the very ancient church he was replacing – his design echoes medieval design and implies longevity and tradition.

OPPOSITE: Detail of the west front.

The diocese was established in an area with a strong Methodist tradition, and today both Anglicans and Methodists work closely together as a Christian witness in Cornwall.

The oldest site of continuous Christian worship in Britain

St Albans Abbey

Site of St Alban's burial around 300;
Benedictine monastery rebuilt 1077–1100; became a cathedral in 1877
www.stalbanscathedral.org

AROUND THE END of the third century AD, nearly 300 years before St Augustine arrived in Canterbury, St Alban, Britain's first Christian martyr, was beheaded near here for giving shelter to a Christian priest, St Amphibalus. A small church was soon established, which was raised to a Benedictine abbey by King Offa in 795. Much of the present building dates to the Norman rebuilding in 1077 by Abbot Paul of Caen, a contemporary and friend of Archbishop Lanfranc of Canterbury.

Unlike Lanfranc, Abbot Paul did not have access to fine French stone: he used recycled brick from the ruins of the Roman city of Verulamium, still visible at the foot of the hill. The abbey was the premier monastery in England until the Dissolution; the shrines of St Alban and St Amphibalus were destroyed in 1539. A reconstruction of St Alban's shrine was completed in 1993 and there are plans to refurbish that of St Amphibalus. Each June St Alban's martyrdom is re-enacted at a festival pilgrimage.

The building was at risk through most of the nineteenth century, following the partial collapse of the south nave wall in 1832 and the threatened collapse of the tower in 1870. Millionaire Lord Grimthorpe came to the rescue but, disliking the Perpendicular style, he controversially insisted on his own designs to replace the west front and the main windows in the transepts, despite having no architectural training.

However, much of the medieval wall decoration survives remarkably well, its soft terracotta and ochre tones complemented by a set of new pulpitum statues by sculptor Rory Young commemorating modern martyrs.

ABOVE: Recycled Roman bricks and Saxon piers in the Norman church.

OPPOSITE: Painted ceiling decoration in the presbytery and crossing and nave beyond.

An immense Gothic cathedral for the troubled twentieth century

Liverpool Cathedral

Designed by Sir Giles Gilbert Scott and built 1904–78
www.liverpoolcathedral.org.uk

LIVERPOOL BECAME THE CITY for a new diocese in 1880, but initially had no cathedral. Its second bishop, Francis James Chavasse, held a competition in 1902 to design it, which was won by the 22-year-old Giles Gilbert Scott, who spent the rest of his life building a massive Gothic sandstone cathedral on high ground overlooking the Mersey.

Scott first built the Lady Chapel. It was designed in the Decorated style and finished in intricate Edwardian Arts and Crafts detailing with the angels making music around the triforium (illustrated on page 6). Because of Scott's youth all this early work required approval of Victorian Gothic Revival architect George Bodley. But after Bodley's death in 1907, Scott's idiom became much more stripped down as he completed first the choir, then the massive central space and finally the nave.

Liverpool Cathedral, like Guildford after it, was a people's cathedral funded by locals, in this case from the Empire's great port city. But the Second World War took its toll on the half-completed building, making the accomplishment even greater. It is the only cathedral in which a war memorial chapel, built after the First World War, is integral to the building. 40,000 Liverpudlians died during that war including the bishop's son, Noel, the only man awarded the Victoria Cross twice in the conflict.

OPPOSITE: Light disappears in the immense height of the interior spaces.

Like the medieval Gothic builders before him, in Liverpool Cathedral Scott achieves great soaring heights and a breathtaking sense of space, combined with beautiful craftsmanship. I particularly love the Arts and Crafts ironwork door and chest hinges in the forms of animals – deer, salamanders and snails – all creating an earthly glimpse of heaven. And if that doesn't do it for you, look inside the west end at Tracey Emin's pink neon handwritten spiritual moment, 'I felt you and I knew you loved me.'

Beautiful parish church cathedral for a great mercantile city

Newcastle Cathedral

Mostly fourteenth-century; became a cathedral in 1882
www.stnicholascathedral.co.uk

NEWCASTLE HAS BEEN A happening place since William the Conqueror's eldest son erected the 'new castle' at the place where Roman Emperor Hadrian had built a bridge across the Tyne. It is a mercantile, seafaring city, so its parish church, a stone's throw from the castle, was dedicated to St Nicholas, patron saint of sailors as well as children. Today the cathedral is generally known as St Nicholas's Cathedral (or 'St Nick's') to distinguish it from the Catholic cathedral in the same city.

By the fifteenth century Newcastle burgers had created a long, low church, the fourth largest parish church in England, with no less than eighteen altars. The beautiful open lantern tower, over 200 feet high, was built in the fifteenth century and was used as a beacon by sailors. Apart from raising the level of the choir and installing fine wooden canons' stalls, carved by local craftsman Ralph Hedley after St Nicholas's became a cathedral in 1882, the church has been little altered since late medieval times.

Like Salisbury in the 1780s, St Nick's had its monuments removed in a perhaps overzealous act of clearing up, but set in front of the west entrance is a fine early fifteenth-century marble font and intricately carved canopy on a pulley. The font cover was saved from threatened destruction by the Reformation and the Scots by being hidden for 150 years. The cathedral also has an exceptionally rich collection of ledger stones, many of them hidden under the platforms when the pews were installed in the late nineteenth century. These are due to be conserved, and the stories of the people they record better told, as part of an ambitious project to reveal old Newcastle with the cathedral at its centre.

OPPOSITE: Buildings up close to St Nick's Cathedral.

BELOW: The font with its cover reinstalled.

Home to the Leaves of Southwell, pinnacle of the medieval mason's art

Southwell Minster

Church of Norman origins from 1108; made a cathedral in 1884
www.southwellminster.org

SOUTHWELL MINSTER, for over 900 years a collegiate minster church, has since 1884 been the mother church of the most southerly diocese in the province of York. Lying close to several Roman roads, the minster is built over a Roman villa and buildings that served as churches since Roman times. Today it is the most easy-to-read Norman cathedral, with no cloisters or other ancillary buildings. (The adjacent Archbishop of York's palace was erected after 1360 and was where Cardinal Wolsey spent his penultimate night.) The nave, transepts and west end, with their distinctive pepper-pot towers, date from the early twelfth century. Inside, the massive piers and three arcades of the Norman nave cannot fail to impress. As elsewhere, the modest apsidal Norman choir was replaced after 1234 by an Early English choir and later a crocketed, ogee-arched, Decorated pulpitum dividing the choir from the nave.

Southwell's masterpiece is the design and decoration of the octagonal chapter house and the passage leading to it, constructed in the last decades of the thirteenth century. The chapter house has no central column; its stone vault is held up by supporting ribs in the shape of a star. Most remarkable are the carved stone decorations on the capitals of every pier, in the bosses, in every gable and sometimes escaping across adjacent columns and spaces. These intricately carved 'Leaves of Southwell' are a celebration of creation, with animals and dragons, human heads and green men, and at least twelve different types of leaf, including oak, hawthorn and buttercup, all deeply and crisply carved with exuberance and great discipline.

OPPOSITE: The Leaves of Southwell: pigs foraging under oak leaves, 1290s.

Thriving city-centre cathedral

Wakefield Cathedral

Restored medieval parish church; became a cathedral in 1888
www.wakefieldcathedral.org.uk

WAKEFIELD'S MEDIEVAL PARISH CHURCH was raised to cathedral status in 1888, then extended and altered by John Loughborough Pearson. The 'new' church was consecrated in 1905. The church actually sits on top of a Saxon foundation, remains of which were discovered during Pearson's works – a church in this location is mentioned in the Domesday Book. Slightly strangely, the land to build the later Norman church was given to Lewes Priory in Sussex by William II in 1090. Sadly almost nothing of this remains, and the current church owes much of its early nineteenth-century appearance to restoration works by Sir George Gilbert Scott and his son John Oldrid Scott between 1858 and 1874. There are interesting roof bosses and an elaborately carved screen. The rood above the screen was designed by Sir Ninian Comper and is very lovely.

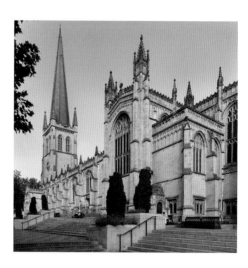

In 2012, after over one hundred years as a cathedral, Wakefield undertook a major renewal programme. The Victorian pews were removed and a Yorkshire stone floor was created, which included a new labyrinth and under-floor heating. Such interventions are inevitably controversial, but for Wakefield it was part of making the cathedral an attractive and vibrant place for worship and Christian mission. The revived popularity of the cathedral for everything from services to concerts, ceilidhs to art projects, demonstrates how successful this has been.

OPPOSITE: The refurbished nave, with labyrinth and restored font.

A baroque jewel in the heart of the Midlands

Birmingham Cathedral

Early eighteenth century church; made a cathedral in 1905
www.birminghamcathedral.com

St Philip's, Birmingham became a cathedral in 1905 and is 300 years old in 2015. It is an eighteenth-century church in the baroque style, with an Italianate influence that sets it apart from medieval churches. It was built by distinguished local architect, Thomas Archer, who also designed St John's, Smith Square, London and parts of Chatsworth House. It sits in its own small park, the only green space in the city centre.

Perhaps the most celebrated elements in Birmingham Cathedral are the four windows by leading Pre-Raphaelite artist and designer Sir Edward Burne-Jones. Burne-Jones was Birmingham-born and baptised in the cathedral. He designed one west-end and three east-end windows specifically for St Philip's, using his signature colours and style. Even on a dull day they are markedly arresting, and in sunshine they are truly breathtaking.

As a city-centre landmark, the cathedral's square is enjoyed by some 20,000 people passing through daily. The park is also used for charity and arts events.

ABOVE: Beyond the choir is Sir Edward Burne-Jones's east window of the Ascension.

OPPOSITE: Detail of the Last Judgment window by Burne-Jones.

Unusually for a cathedral, Birmingham retains some of its original box pews and its original eighteenth-century wrought iron screen. Designed and built as the church for what was becoming a major town, it retains a strong local flavour, including memorials to events such as the 1974 Birmingham pub bombings. More happily, it is often used to exhibit art and sculpture, making it an ever-changing space.

'Overie' home to actors, writers, brewers, merchants and traders

Southwark Cathedral

Early Gothic church for London; created a cathedral in 1905
cathedral.southwark.anglican.org

THE CHURCH SITS ON A SITE that may have been a Roman temple and, from 606, a convent. The Normans established an Augustinian priory and, following a fire in 1212, one of the earliest churches to be built in the Early English Gothic style. It was dedicated to St Mary and became known as St Mary Overie (Old English for 'over the river'). After the Dissolution, it was converted into a parish church, which in later years suffered from neglect, proximity to railways and road-building.

In the nineteenth century Sir Arthur Blomfield and later Sir Ninian Comper restored and beautified the building, and recently the cathedral has shared in the revival of the area along with Borough Market, Shakespeare's recreated Globe Theatre and Tate Modern. Shakespeare's brother is buried here. The playwright possibly introduced John Harvard's parents to each other. Harvard, who granted a legacy to the American university bearing his name, is commemorated in a chapel at the cathedral. Chaucer's pilgrims set out from the Tabard Inn nearby, and Charles Dickens wrote in his journals about visiting the bell-ringers here.

ABOVE: Memorial to William Shakespeare by Henry McCarthy, 1912.

The district has long-standing medical connections. St Thomas's Hospital was originally established by the Augustinians, and dedicated to Thomas Becket. There are also historic connections with Guy's Hospital, continuing to the present. St Andrew's Chapel in the cathedral is set aside to support those struggling with AIDS and HIV.

I particularly love the seventeenth-century chandelier hanging from the central crossing. It has a crown (representing the king) hanging above a mitre (church), showing who was boss. It was given by a local woman whose husband had bought their inn from the Harvard family.

Transformed by Dykes Bower in Gothic Revival style

St Edmundsbury Cathedral

Parish church; became a cathedral in 1914
www.stedscathedral.co.uk

A YEAR BEFORE the Norman Conquest, work started on a huge Benedictine abbey dedicated to Edmund, the Saxon king of East Anglia who was martyred by the Danes in 869 and who gives his name to the cathedral and to the town of Bury St Edmunds. At 500 feet long, the abbey boasted one of the largest churches in England. However amid the destruction of the Dissolution the abbey church and complex were plundered for their building materials. St James's Church, one of three great churches within the abbey precinct, was retained as the parish church. It was constructed from 1503 by John Wastell, who also designed the fan vaulting at nearby King's College Chapel, Cambridge.

St James's became a cathedral in 1914, and the building we see today owes much to its later twentieth-century architect and benefactor, Stephen Dykes Bower, who worked firmly in the tradition of the nineteenth-century Gothic Revival. He added first the east end and one range of cloisters. The Cathedral Centre was built in 1990. His legacy paid for the magnificent crossing tower, which was constructed to his design and sits proud above the surrounding roofs like the towers and spires in the Suffolk countryside around. The tower, completed for the Millennium, floods the building with light and its more recent fan-vaulted painted ceiling sparkles like a jewel box. This brightly-coloured design can be found decorating everything from cathedral jams to carrier bags.

Dykes Bower had a wonderful eye for detail and he also designed the Transfiguration Chapel in the north-east of the building, delineated by an unusual simplified massive arcade. It is a serene setting in which to contemplate Dame Elisabeth Frink's *Crucifixion*.

ABOVE: The Norman gate and belfry, with the cathedral beyond.

OPPOSITE: Painted tower vaulting, completed in 2010 to Stephen Dykes Bower's design.

A jewel box of contemporary art

Chelmsford Cathedral

Fifteenth-century parish church; became a cathedral in 1914
www.chelmsfordcathedral.org.uk

ST MARY'S PARISH CHURCH, in its compact green churchyard, became Chelmsford Cathedral in 1914. Grand designs by Sir Charles Nicholson, who extended Portsmouth Cathedral in the early twentieth century, never materialised. Indeed, perhaps the most significant intervention in the last 100 years has been the 1983 refurbishment that removed much woodwork and installed a luminous French limestone floor with a boldness that probably wouldn't be allowed today.

The effect is a wonderfully light and colourful interior enhanced by a series of new art commissions. So effective are these that former *Times* journalist Ruth Gledhill describes Chelmsford as 'a stunningly beautiful and spacious white interior. This cathedral stands as one of the hidden glories of the Church of England.'

Beryl Dean's brightly coloured patchwork at the east end representing the churches of the diocese sets a colourful tone. The colour is picked up in stained glass, icons and Mark Cazalet's gorgeous figurative painting in the north transept of *The Tree of Life*, which also reminds us of our responsibilities to the environment.

To celebrate the cathedral's centenary Mark Cazalet engraved a clear-glassed window with the figure of St Cedd, seventh-century bishop of the East Saxons. Elsewhere Peter Sanderson's tapestry altar frontal depicts the sea and the isolated Saxon chapel of St Peter Bradwell which was built by St Cedd. It is a contemplative work heavily reminiscent of the flat Essex coast.

Recently the Dean has introduced collegiate-style seating (with the congregation facing each other) enhancing the sense of space and inclusiveness as well as showcasing the painted, gilded nave ceiling (right). His desire to create a place for connection is well served.

OPPOSITE: *The Tree of Life* by Mark Cazalet. Below it is *The Living Cross* by Helen McIldowie-Jenkins.

From Anglo-Saxon art to modern worship

Sheffield Cathedral

Enlarged medieval church; became a cathedral in 1914
www.sheffieldcathedral.org

THE CATHEDRAL CHURCH of St Peter and St Paul dates from around 1430, but a chance discovery in a cutler's workshop in Sheffield put the date of Christian worship on this site back to as early as the ninth century. The Anglo-Saxon Sheffield Cross, a beautifully carved stone high cross, now sits in the British Museum, and is thought to have been the rood of the original church.

The discovery of crucible steel in the 1740s transformed Sheffield's fortunes and population. Consequently the church has been much altered: the nave was rebuilt in Victorian times, and chapels and the chapter house were added before the Second World War, after the church was elevated to cathedral status.

Magnificent medieval tomb monuments have been preserved in the Shrewsbury and Lady Chapels and elsewhere are memorials to the six Sheffield Worthies and the servicemen and women of Sheffield. The 1960s saw a narthex entrance to the extended west end and a lantern tower to bring light to the cathedral. In 1999 this was filled with an abstract stained-glass design by Amber Hiscott.

The focus has recently shifted, with a large Heritage Lottery Fund project to improve access and better integrate the church into its local surroundings, allowing it to play a greater civic role alongside its continuing tradition of worship. The Gateway Project, completed in 2014, includes a welcoming new entrance and improved heating, flooring and seating inside. At the west end is a new stainless-steel font by Brian Fell.

ABOVE: Dappled sunshine on the nave and the new, light oak benches by Luke Hughes.

OPPOSITE: The lantern tower from below.

Destruction, reconciliation, peace and rebirth

Coventry Cathedral

Modern cathedral of 1962, adjoining its devastated medieval predecessor
www.coventrycathedral.org.uk

COVENTRY IS A UNIQUE SITE in that it has two consecrated cathedral buildings, albeit one is in ruins. The original pre-Reformation cathedral, St Mary's, now an archaeological site, lost its official cathedral status after the Dissolution. This status was restored in 1918 and the parish church of St Michael's, one of the largest in England, became Coventry's cathedral. Just 22 years later, after a Luftwaffe raid on 14 November 1940, that building was left nothing more than a shell.

The determination to create something new out of the rubble was instant and indomitable; by 1962 a new cathedral had been built, incorporating the shell of old St Michael's as part of the new setting.

It was decided to design the new cathedral as a homage to the twentieth century, reflecting the period in which the devastation took place, and the good that could also come from the age. The Basil Spence design took just six years to build. Set at right angles to the old ruins, it is the most modern cathedral in England. Among its many stunning treasures are the external sculpture of St Michael, a powerful avenging angel by Sir Jacob Epstein, and *Christ in Majesty* by Graham Sutherland, the largest tapestry in the world, which adorns the east end. John Piper's stained glass dazzles in the building that has become the centre for the Anglican mission towards peace and reconciliation. It was a fitting setting for the première of Benjamin Britten's *War Requiem* in 1962, a piece specially commissioned for the new cathedral.

OPPOSITE: John Piper window in the baptistry of the new cathedral.

Ancient and modern, hidden gem of Yorkshire

Bradford Cathedral

Fifteenth-century church with 1950s extensions by Sir Edward Maufe
www.bradfordcathedral.org

BRADFORD IS A grand Victorian city with impressive nineteenth-century buildings built on the textile boom. Sitting on a grassy rise overlooking the centre, Bradford's medieval parish church gained cathedral status in 1919.

The fifteenth-century tower, easily visible from the town, and the nave, filled with a warm light from the clerestory windows most times of the day, are the oldest parts of the cathedral. The medieval church is now flanked by fine wings and an east-end extension of the 1950s and 1960s designed by Sir Edward Maufe, the architect of Guildford Cathedral. Maufe had to build on a tight site and achieved a sense of depth in the Lady Chapel through using tall but narrow arches. The massing of the extensions is in scale with the earlier building and creates a harmony between old and new.

Bradford Cathedral enjoys extensive nineteenth- and twentieth-century stained glass, including by the Arts and Crafts firm Morris & Co. Bradford-born Ernst Sichel's World War One Memorial Window to the left of the north door graphically tells the stories of the West Yorkshire regiment – landing in France, fighting on the Somme and arriving in 1919 in Cologne. Most recently textile artist Polly Meynell has produced a bold set of seasonal altar frontals.

In 2011 Bradford was awarded Eco-Congregation status and became the first cathedral to generate its own energy though solar panels on the south roof. Now work is beginning to conserve the grand nineteenth-century State Gate, which faces the new Westfield shopping centre being built as this proud city reenergises itself.

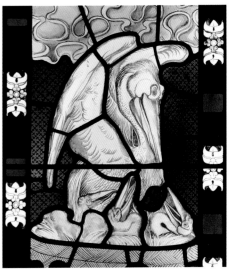

ABOVE: 'Pelican in her Piety', stained-glass detail by Philip Webb for Morris & Co.

From Gothic Revival to modern work of art

Blackburn Cathedral

1820s parish church; made a cathedral in 1926
www.blackburncathedral.com

BUILT BY JOHN PALMER in 1826, the parish church
of St Mary the Virgin was designated a cathedral
a century later with the creation of the diocese
of Blackburn. It combines the original 1820s
structure with 1950s and 1960s modernist
additions, including the distinctive aluminium
spire by the architect Laurence King. This
unusual mix of ancient and modern, echoed in
some other parish church cathedrals such as
Bradford, give the building the size and dignity
worthy of a cathedral.

Of the Gothic Revival elements from the
original design, perhaps the most notable are
the magnificent roof bosses. The wonderful
twentieth-century corona over the high altar
marks out the holy space within what is largely
an open and light building, imparting a sense of
gravitas, whilst the equally modern font provides
a liturgical welcome in the south transept, which
will soon become a new major entrance.

The cathedral is working in partnership with
the local borough council and the Homes and
Communities Agency on the multi-million pound
Cathedral Quarter regeneration project, which
will include this new entrance and a cloister with associated
housing. This will provide the town with the centre it deserves – a
place of beauty, respite, worship and entertainment which is open
to all. In this sense Blackburn Cathedral continues to be a modern
and forward-thinking place, dedicated to its local community.

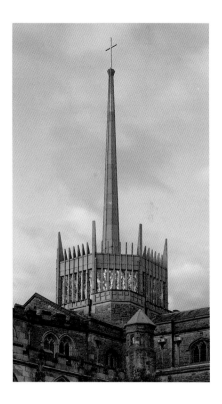

ABOVE: Illuminated corona
with aluminium spire.

Transformed by the Industrial Revolution

Derby Cathedral

Gibbs's church of the Enlightenment, with a sixteenth-century tower; made a cathedral in 1927

www.derbycathedral.org

THE TOWN OF DERBY became prosperous almost overnight with the Enlightenment, when it witnessed the first stirrings of the Industrial Revolution. Close to the church was Britain's earliest factory, a water-powered silk mill. The tombstone of local painter Joseph Wright of Derby is mounted on the wall. Wright mixed with other influential eighteenth-century scientists, intellectuals and industrialists and is famous for his paintings of industrial experiments.

In the 1720s the parishioners pulled down their church, leaving only the fine 1530s tower (right), and with their new industrial wealth James Gibbs built a broad single-storey church with large round-headed windows that still flood the church with light and confidence. Later the Industrial Revolution moved elsewhere, though wealth returned in the nineteenth century, in part from the railways, and Derby Parish Church became a cathedral in 1927.

Just as in Gibbs's St Martin-in-the-Fields, London, tall Doric columns divide the nave from the aisles and ground the undulating groin vaulting. Most exquisite is the 1730s gilded wrought iron screen by local smith Robert Bakewell. Traversing the whole church, it has been described as 'delicate as lace and intricate as a fugue'. The screen's blue and gold are picked up in Ceri Richards's twentieth-century stained-glass windows.

OPPOSITE: Robert Bakewell's screen (1730s) embellishes the interior.

In the late 1960s Sebastian Comper added the retro choir, designed by his father Sir Ninian Comper, that harmonises well with Gibbs's building. Four-times-married Bess of Hardwick has a monument in the church, setting a trend for later Cavendishes including Georgiana, Duchess of Devonshire.

The resting place of the last Plantagenet king

Leicester Cathedral

Medieval parish church; hallowed as Leicester Cathedral in 1927
leicestercathedral.org

THE CHURCH OF ST MARTIN has seen much change and growth over the years. Its interior woodwork scheme was designed by Sir Charles Nicholson, who worked on several other twentieth-century cathedrals; the great east window, designed by Christopher Whall, commemorates those who perished in the First World War; and the Vaughan Porch was designed by John Loughborough Pearson.

The discovery in 2012 of the mortal remains of King Richard III beneath a car park directly opposite the cathedral has led to a resurgence of interest in the site. Following a radical transformation of the surrounding precincts, Cathedral Gardens were opened in July 2014, creating an attractive open space at the heart of the city, and linking the cathedral to the new Richard III Visitor Centre. The remains of the king himself were reinterred in Leicester Cathedral in March 2015, within a newly created ambulatory space towards the east end of the cathedral designed by Josh McCosh. For my children a visit to the cathedral and the visitor centre during a wet half term brought royal medieval history to life.

Leicester Cathedral has strong links to its surrounding community: services and events are regularly held in partnership with local charities and faith communities; outreach programmes run from the neighbouring St Martin's House provide support for the vulnerable and needy; and a strong choral tradition continues to be developed through the cathedral's diocesan schools' singing programme *DioSing!*

OPPOSITE: The bronze statue commemorating Richard III by James Walter Butler (1980) was moved to the Cathedral Gardens in 2014.

The cathedral of the sea

Portsmouth Cathedral

Norman church with seventeenth-century revisions; became a cathedral in 1927
www.portsmouthcathedral.org.uk

THE CHURCH OF THOMAS of Canterbury was built in Portsmouth around 1190 by a friend of St Thomas Becket, the Archbishop of Canterbury who was scandalously murdered in his cathedral in 1170 by King Henry II's men. Recently two fragments of the saint's skull were donated to the cathedral. Much of the fine medieval church remains at the east end. Disruption in the Civil War resulted in the rebuilding of the nave and a large lantern was constructed over the crossing tower in the late seventeenth century.

Taller than other buildings in old Portsmouth, the lantern acted as a beacon to sailors. Many famous and more obscure travellers set sail from Portsmouth over the centuries. Consequently the cathedral is full of references to the sea, including the grave of a crew member from Henry VIII's naval flagship warship the *Mary Rose*, as well as touching memorials to those who have lost their lives in recent shipping accidents.

After the church was elevated to cathedral status, Sir Charles Nicholson commenced an ambitious rebuilding of the nave in a striking, massive Byzantine style. Building works stopped during the Second World War. Finally, in the early 1990s Michael Drury completed the west end with two pepper-pot towers in a continental Romanesque style complementing Nicholson's nave. Throughout the cathedral is infused with light, in both the massive twentieth-century nave and the medieval east end, where the tightly-stacked seventeenth-century box pews have been cut back or removed. This might raise eyebrows today, but it does create a wonderfully open space.

ABOVE: The cathedral's Golden Barque weathervane, dating from 1710.

The People's Cathedral

Guildford Cathedral

Designed by Sir Edward Maufe and built 1936–39 and 1952–61
www.guildford-cathedral.org

THE DIOCESE OF GUILDFORD was created out of the large medieval diocese of Winchester in 1927. As the site of Guildford parish church was deemed too small, Stag Hill, an undeveloped site outside the town, was given for the building of a cathedral by Lord Onslow. A competition was held for the design of the new cathedral, which was won by Sir Edward Maufe. Construction started in 1932 but progress was halted by the War. Building continued in the 1950s and the chancel and crossing were complete by 1954. The cathedral was consecrated in the presence of the Queen in 1961.

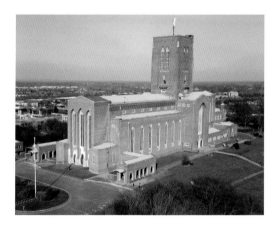

Thus Guildford is just over 50 years old, and so many still remember how it came into being. The cathedral is built of brick and in the 1950s the Queen, my mother, who was then a schoolgirl, and many others contributed 2s 6d (12.5p) to the 'Buy a Brick' campaign to build the cathedral.

The brief was 'to produce a design, definitely of our time, yet in the line of the great cathedrals, to build anew on tradition'. Maufe did indeed build in the Gothic manner, putting great emphasis on space, light, massing and soaring vertical heights but in a twentieth-century idiom and experimenting with twentieth-century building techniques such as high-level, in-situ cast concrete.

OPPOSITE: Sir Edward Maufe's expression of light and spaciousness in the nave.

Ever since its opening the cathedral has been a landmark visible for miles away, especially from the A3 that curves around it – it is the only Church of England cathedral designed to be approached by car – and it marked the end of my journey around the great cathedral churches of the Church of England.

A FINAL WORD ON FUNDING

CATHEDRALS ARE THE most significant buildings within England's wonderful architectural heritage. They are also among the most expensive to maintain. Benefaction to cathedrals is as old as the buildings themselves. And indeed the names of distant medieval donors are often reflected in the very fabric. Sir Thomas Erpingham's benefaction to Norwich Cathedral in the fourteenth century is, for example, commemorated in the cathedral's Erpingham Gate.

The motivation of those contributing to religious buildings in the medieval period may be considerably different to contemporary donors, but the need for charitable funding remains great. The government provides no ongoing support for the maintenance of these expensive buildings. Recognising that much of the strain must therefore be taken by private philanthropy, the Wolfson Foundation in 2011 established a Cathedral Fabric Repair Fund in partnership with the Cathedrals Fabric Commission and fellow funders, the Pilgrim Trust. This successful partnership funded essential work at the majority of England's cathedrals.

Much of the recent investment in cathedrals has, reasonably enough, been to create exciting new facilities, such as education or exhibition centres (often encouraged by the Heritage Lottery Fund). But the Cathedral Fabric Repair Fund deliberately funded crucial but relatively unglamorous work to roofs or to stonework: essential to make the building safe and to pass it securely to another generation, but all too easy to ignore when funding is tight. And so it has been extremely heartening that, partially on the back of the Fund, in 2014 the government allocated £20 million for repair work as part of the First World War centenary commemorations. In doing so, they recognise the importance of these noble buildings in helping the country remember the cost of war.

Philanthropy is often seen as the pursuit of individuals or organisations able to donate significant sums of money. In reality, the funding of cathedrals is a partnership between many different types of funders, ranging from foundations able to give multi-million pound grants to the worshipping community contributing on a collection plate. And, ideally, it is – and will remain – a partnership between government funding and charitable money.

PAUL RAMSBOTTOM
Chief Executive, Wolfson Foundation

ARCHITECTURAL STYLES

The following are the main defining features of styles found in English church architecture. The dates are approximate and overlapping, with new styles being introduced in some locations while older styles persisted in others.

Norman or English Romanesque, 1066–1190
Style originating in Normandy and introduced to England on a wide scale following the Norman Conquest. It features massive round columns, high thick stone walls and round-topped arches, often with bands of simple incised zig-zag patterning. The cruciform church with a square crossing tower became common in this period.

English Gothic, 1175–1540
The Gothic style was a new influence from France, characterised by pointed arches, soaring heights, thinner, pierced walls and the use of light to penetrate the building, often coloured through magnificent new stained-glass windows. In England the Gothic style developed distinctively in three phases:

Early English Gothic, 1175–1265
The main change was the introduction of pointed arches and narrow, pointed lancet windows, rather than the round-headed Norman arch. These enabled taller buildings and larger windows to be constructed.

Decorated Gothic, 1250–1370
Over time tracery in the windows and other decorative features became more complicated and curvilinear, evolving into what is called the Decorated style, characterised by elaborate window tracery, more slender columns and the use of decorative ribbed vaulting.

Perpendicular Gothic, 1330–1540
Unique to England, the Perpendicular style featured strong grids of vertical and horizontal lines, huge window surfaces, and even more elaborate vaulting, culminating in the fan vault.

Baroque, 1666–1730s
Originating in late sixteenth-century Italy, the Baroque developed Roman-derived Renaissance styles into imposingly theatrical church buildings strongly associated with the Catholic Counter-Reformation. As such it had little influence in Protestant England until Sir Christopher Wren's restrained use of the style for St Paul's Cathedral and his other rebuilt churches in the City of London.

Gothic Revival or Neo-Gothic, 1745–
Associated with the Romantic movement of the mid-eighteenth century was a greater appreciation of medieval arts and craftsmanship. This developed into an architectural movement strongly associated with the Anglo-Catholic movement of the Church of England. Numerous new churches and additions to existing churches were built in Gothic style in England's expanding industrial towns and cities during the nineteenth century and continued alongside throughout the twentieth: the tower at St Edmundsbury Cathedral was completed only in 2005.

First published in 2015 by Scala Arts & Heritage Publishers Ltd
10 Lion Yard, Tremadoc Road, London SW4 7NQ, UK
www.scalapublishers.com

In association with Cathedral and Church Buildings Division
Archbishops' Council, The Church of England
Church House, Great Smith Street, London SW1P 3AZ
www.ChurchCare.co.uk

Designed by Nigel Soper; project managed by Oliver Craske
ISBN: 978-1-85759-940-4; printed in India 10 9 8 7 6 5 4 3 2 1

ACKNOWLEDGEMENTS

JANET GOUGH WOULD LIKE TO THANK the Deans and Chapters of the
42 cathedrals of the Church of England; the Association of English
Cathedrals; the Rt Hon Frank Field MP, Jennie Page CBE and the
Cathedrals Fabric Commission for England; Becky Clark, Anne
Locke, Rhiannon Wicks and the Cathedral and Church Buildings
Division; the Rt Revd Dr John Inge, Bishop of Worcester; Paul
Ramsbottom, Chief Executive, the Wolfson Foundation; Georgina
Naylor, Director, the Pilgrim Trust; Ian Morrison and the Heritage
Lottery Fund; Beth McHattie; Sir Paul Ruddock; Oliver Craske;
Jim, Tom and Alice Lloyd and Sparky.

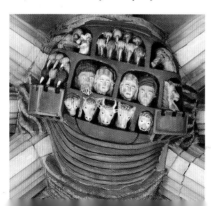

PICTURE CREDITS

All photographs by Paul Barker / © Archbishops'
Council except: 2–3, 11: Photo Robert Greshoff
/ © Robert Greshoff & Cathedral Enterprises
Ltd; 4, 14–15: Winchester Cathedral; 5, 39: Wells
Cathedral; 8, 34–35: Chichester Cathedral; 9:
Graham Lacdao, courtesy of St Paul's Cathedral;
10: © The Stained Glass Studio at Canterbury
Cathedral; 18: Durham Cathedral; 19: Angelo
Hornak; 20: Angelo Hornak/Ely Cathedral; 21: Ely
Cathedral; 22–23, 96: Copyright Paul Hurst; 26:
York Minster; 27: York Glaziers Trust, reproduced
courtesy of the Chapter of York; 28: Lincoln
Cathedral; 29: Bryan Hamilton (bryan666uk on
Flickr); 30: John Crook; 31: Ash Mills (www.
ashmills.com); 38: Jonathan Sawyer; 40: Digitally
enhanced image of Mappa Mundi by the Folio
Society, reproduced by permission of the Dean
and Chapter of Hereford and the Hereford Mappa
Mundi Trust; 41: Gordon Taylor, reproduced by
permission of the Dean and Chapter of Hereford;
42–43: Peterborough Cathedral; 44–45: Christ
Church Cathedral, Oxford; 46: Gloucester
Cathedral; 47: Angelo Hornak, reproduced
by permission of Gloucester Cathedral; 48:
Bristol Cathedral; 49: Jon Cannon; 52–53:
Jonathan Buckmaster; 56–57: Angelo Hornak/
Manchester Cathedral; 58: Truro Cathedral;
59: Paul Richards/Truro Cathedral 60–61:
Donato Cinicolo; 64: Robyn Frame; 65: © www.
webbaviation.co.uk; 72–73: Southwark Cathedral;
74–75: St Edmundsbury Cathedral; 80: Coventry
Cathedral; 81: © Coventry Cathedral, photo by
Timothy Eccleston; 82–83: Bradford Cathedral;
84–85: Angelo Hornak, reproduced by permission
of Blackburn Cathedral; 86–87: Derby Cathedral;
88–89: Dean and Chapter of Leicester Cathedral;
92: © David Hogg; 93: Guildford Cathedral

With thanks to the Wolfson Foundation for
sponsoring new photographs by Paul Barker.

LEFT: Ceiling boss of Noah's Ark from Norwich
Cathedral.